CW00927225

SCIENCE

THE NEW GOD?

by Easton Hamilton

A TRIBUTE

All three books in this trilogy (of which this is the first) are dedicated to my late, beloved wife, Deborah Hamilton.... She left such a beautiful legacy, far more than I can document here. I will always be grateful to her for her unwavering support, love and friendship over twenty-seven years.

During the last seven and a half years of her life, when Deborah knew she was dying, she became a beautiful example of how to live life whilst knowing death was inevitable. She spent those years using the challenge of her experience to uplift and inspire others, even though she was the one facing a terminal illness. During this time, in fact, within hours of her final moments, Deborah told me to be aware that there was 'something' I was going to need to do. She told me that I wouldn't need to look for it because it would come and find me and that our journey together, especially the final chapter, would be invaluable in helping me to complete that something. I now know that this trilogy (which includes: Science... The New God? and Synergy: the cure for all ills) is part of the task she was referring to and that the rest of this revelation is still quietly unfolding and will come to fruition soon.

Deborah, I want to take this opportunity to thank you for the courage, dignity and grace that you exemplified in life and especially as you were meeting your end. Through the way you lived you taught me how to embrace life and also how to meet death. You also taught me how to be peaceful, stable and content in the face of difficulty; you always did this with such humour and a warm, enigmatic smile. I will keep your legacy with me and endeavour to live my life inspired by those values and virtues.

The beautiful foundation you laid for our children has ensured they continue to blossom. They are both fragrant flowers in the garden of life. There are not enough words to reflect my love, admiration and respect for you. This work, which is an attempt to expand hearts and minds, has been done in part to honour the way you lived your life and the pursuit of truth which was so sacred to you. I hope it will do your memory justice. Thank you for the example of your honesty, courage and integrity. Peace be with you always.

In love and eternal friendship

Easton xx

CONTENTS

PREFACE
SCIENCE: THE NEW GOD?

This book forms part of a trilogy (the other two in the series are Antiquity Comes Full Circle and Synergy: The Cure for All Ills. Science: The New God? is a small attempt to challenge the notion that science and progress generally have all been to our advantage. It dares to question science's supremacy in our modern world, because we now appear to live in a world where, unless something is endorsed by science, its value and validity is questioned, and it is my belief that we should at least be questioning this premise. Does science have all the answers? Should it be our primary source of reference when drawing conclusions? Is it really the ultimate arbiter? Hopefully, you will be better able to answer these questions for yourself at the end of this journey.

There is no doubt that we owe science much because it has enabled us to cross so many bridges, in fields such as medicine, the environmental sciences, information technology, all aspects of engineering and much more. And yet almost simultaneously, whilst opening our minds to new frontiers, it has closed the door on many of the 'softer sciences', calling their credibility into question. Many would say these subjects have little place in the modern world, and belong to a time when we were more ignorant, less evolved. The softer sciences could be described as: spirituality, alternative and complementary medicines and those disciplines that belong to the mind-body and holistic traditions. But is it fair to condemn softer sciences which in many cases (Ayurvedic medicine, acupuncture, herbalism, Chinese medicine and homeopathy, for instance) have been around and have proven to be effective for centuries? .... This of course is where the debate begins - what does 'proven' mean?

Science has built its reputation on proving or disproving whatever hypotheses it is scrutinising, which is fine, but is hypothesis testing the only way to prove or disprove something? Sir Karl Popper (1902-1995), a philosopher best known for his work concerning the validity of scientific theory, said that science could only disprove 'things', it could not in fact prove them. So maybe science needs to acquire a bit more humility. At times its 'certainty' is worrying especially when you take into account that every 40 years or so science unearths a new point of view, which usually dethrones the previous one. We seem to constantly give science the benefit of the doubt, more readily remembering when science gets things right and forgetting too easily when it gets things wrong. Science: The New God? is not a condemnation of science, because science is invaluable and I accept that it is needed. This work is merely inviting us to question the 'certainty' and sometimes arrogance of science. We need to be careful, as we follow the hypnotic lure of science down its many paths, that we remember how often science has changed its mind over the generations, throwing up a different perspective or point of view in the process. So although it is a wonderful instrument of insight and learning we must not see it as our sole point of reference, otherwise we are in danger of throwing out the baby with the bath water - which in so many instances we have already done! This is why disciplines such as: herbalism, acupuncture, osteopathy, homeopathy to name a few, have all had to fight for a seat at the table of 'truth'. (In this context I am referring to the truth about the human condition and what best serves humanity's evolution.)

Sadly we are still some way off a genuine merger of ideas when it comes to the older theories and concepts being amalgamated to the new emerging sciences. But there are some green shoots of promise with such disciplines as: neurotheology (the bridging of spirituality and science), orthomolecular medicine (using the right nutrients to address biological dysfunctions), epigenetics (exposing that we are more than our genetic material) and psychoneuroimmunology (the science of how thoughts and feelings affect the immune and central nervous systems). These are just a few disciplines that are developing alongside the advancements in neuro-biology/psychology, and which are changing our understanding of what it is to be human. They are also helping us to see the limitations of a purely scientific view of the world.

If this book does appeal to you I hope you will be inspired to read 'Antiquity Comes Full Circle', where I will take you on a journey back into the past, not for the sake of nostalgia but to help you better understand how we come to be standing where we are right now. It will also help you to understand how we have traded away so much in the name of progress and in doing so have lost so many of our essential core values. Hopefully it will inspire you to take a journey into the future whilst embracing the best of the past. The final piece in the jigsaw is 'Synergy: The Cure for All Ills, which is the most substantial of the three works and covers the eternal principle: "the whole is greater than the sum of its parts". In this book I'll help you to see that healing cannot truly be achieved without adequately addressing: mind, body, spirit and environment. In fact this book goes further, as it throws doubt on any protocol that does not invite the individual seeking help to look at the multi-factorial nature of their condition. It is very rare that the presenting problem is *the* problem. More often than not it is merely the symptom. With the help of this book (Synergy: The Cure for All Ills), you will stop simply putting out fires and be able to persuade the arsonist not to start the fires in the first place!

Hopefully you will be inspired to read the other books in this trilogy, but it is not essential for all three to be read…. you might be only attracted to one, which is absolutely fine as they all stand alone and can be used and enjoyed without reference to each other. I hope you do enjoy this particular journey.

"Not everything that can be counted counts, and not everything that counts can be counted".

Albert Einstein (1879 – 1955)

ACKNOWLEDGMENTS

There are far too many people for me to thank personally because my journey has been such a complex and intricate affair. I've been helped by my friends and enemies alike. My friends have loved me, supported me, encouraged and inspired me. My enemies have taught me to have the courage of my convictions and to practise humility, empathy and compassion. I feel blessed, given my humble beginnings, to have an opportunity to share my insights and experiences in a way that may be useful to those interested in the journey of introspection. So to all my friends, you know who you are, thank you. And to all my enemies, heartfelt thanks to you too.

Thanks also to my Mother and Father, who have supported me emotionally, psychologically and financially over the years and taught me the values of charity and generosity. Thanks to my beautiful children (Rebecca and Earl) who quietly champion me in all that I do. You are both precious and priceless to me. A special mention goes to my sister-in-law (Tracy) whose sacrifice, love and support which she so freely gives to the whole family is truly appreciated by us all.

Special thanks go to Jo Kilburn who gave generously of her time and energy to this project and without her contribution this trilogy would not have happened. The task was also made easier by the contributions of Jocelyne Ansorge and Rashna Walton who patiently looked over my words and offered their proof reading and editing expertise. Special mention goes to Elaine Jackson and Judith Madeley, who've faithfully walked by my side now for many years and have both helped to make Reach an organisation built on conscience and integrity. I am eternally grateful to them all for their love, consistent support and friendship.

Finally I want to thank the (literally) thousands of clients who have inspired me by sharing their hearts and minds in a way that keeps me striving to be the best I can be. I never take their honesty and trust for granted. Thank you.

Easton Hamilton

INTRODUCTION

The immense contribution that science has made to our lives is indisputable. Whatever direction we look in we can see evidence of its awesome power: from the simple battery and light bulb to the vast ocean liners traversing the sea and the incredible, gravity defying, sculpted pieces of metal flying through the skies. So many of science's feats are staggering to such an extent that many of us would now struggle to live our lives without them. But have these technological advances also contributed to distancing us from ourselves? Have we become so dependent on the external comforts and benefits of science that the invisible landscape of the self has not been (and is still not being) fully appreciated or explored? It's my proposition that we have indeed become dependent in this way to such an extent that we live in a 'divided self'. A self that's so busy living up to, or more accurately living down to, the expectations of others and the world, that it's lost sight of itself and of what's really important.

Four hundred years ago, science began to intensify its duel with religion and an era that was more divided in its perception and understanding of the world began to emerge. From that point in (1609) when Galileo peered through a telescope and saw the moon close up, a tug of war between science and religion ensued and the beginnings of a quiet arrogance in the developed world, that somehow because of our science 'we knew better', was born.

It's my hypothesis that this position has not altered. In fact as more discoveries and scientific developments have emerged this arrogance has expanded to such an extent that in some cultures, in some parts of the world, it's fair to say that science has become the new God of our time! We've arrived at a point in history where we now say: "unless it can be scientifically proven it does not exist or at best we should doubt its existence". But is science truly the only measure of reality? In fact, is it a measure we can trust completely? Science's own journey to this point is one of varying theoretical perspectives, being overthrown by new, different hypotheses and discoveries. History is littered with such examples, as I will go on to demonstrate in this narrative.

Let me be clear: I am not suggesting that science doesn't have a place in the modern world or that it should be treated like our enemy. I believe it certainly does have a place but the key word here is 'place'. There's no doubt that science has been a significant contributor to the development of our understanding of the human condition. However, it does not have a monopoly on the truth and therefore should not be seen as the final judge and jury when drawing our conclusions about what's valid or invalid. I believe this is the mistake that has been made and continues to be made and that as a result, spiritual and religious perspectives that are still relevant and useful have been largely demoted over the last 400 years and with that, many of the values and principles that would enrich our lives have been lost.

Is this seemingly lop-sided view of the world one we should trust? Let us explore....

CHAPTER 1:
THE BIRTH OF SCIENCE?

It's difficult to plot the exact moment of the conception of science. There remains some dispute over whether it has always been with us in some social and cultural way and therefore has only latterly been defined as science or whether we can point to a moment in time when science became probably our most important reference point for how we perceive ourselves and the world. There is however sufficient consensus that if there were a moment of birth then it was 400 years ago, in 1609 when Galileo (1564-1642) looked at the moon through a telescope, thereby changing our understanding of the universe forever. This event considered such a moment of significance for the world that some have compared it to the birth of Christ because it was that moment when the impossible entered human affairs. As I've already stated, a point of conception does remain contentious and yet that particular moment was to change the outlook and evolution of the world as we know it.

From Aristotle to Aquinas

The revelations that have followed since Galileo have slowly served to evict God and religion from our understanding of the solar system in which we live. If we look at what existed before Galileo, from the time of Aristotle through to St Thomas Aquinas, we can see that science in that period (which might be described as medieval science) was not divorced from God and religion. There was clearly some accommodation of both material and spiritual aspects. Aristotle was born in 384 BC. He was and remains the very emblem of human wisdom. His style was dispassionate, cool and analytical and his intelligence universal. He brought together physics and cosmology, which became the basis of medieval thought. Although his contribution may in the current light seem strange and even poetic it was based on an extraordinary imagination and on 'the science of the day'. Such was Aristotle's contribution that in the 13th century, Aquinas and the scholastic theologians of the time tried to integrate Aristotelian thought with the triumph of Christianity. St. Thomas Aquinas was concerned with integration and his unfinished work 'Summa Theologica' was an attempt to bring all theories together. It represents the pinnacle of intellectual Christianity. It defined and endorsed Aristotle and established the primary synthesis of the medieval mind by uniting his thought (Aristotle's) with the revelation of Christianity. This was his attempt to put the whole of creation and history into a simple intellectual structure that unified the opposing strands of consciousness that were in danger of challenging the understanding of the day.

It is of course impossible to summarise history entirely in one or two paragraphs, for not only would so much of the relevant detail be lost but many amazing minds and contributors to the story of human kind would not be properly accounted for. Nevertheless, there is immense value in looking at the 'spine' of events that have brought us to this point in time. If we look at what has underpinned so much of our thinking for over the last 2000 years Aristotle's contribution of classical thought has a significant place in the evolution of human kind. Ptolemy, the great astronomer and physicist around AD 150, was amongst the first to suggest that the earth was spherical (although it's not entirely clear whether it was Pythagoras or Aristotle that first proposed this notion). What is clear is that Eratosthenes (the Greek mathematician, astronomer and poet) was the first to accurately measure the diameter of the earth (240 BC). This was a long time before, in 1492, Christopher Columbus courageously tested the hypothesis that the earth was indeed 'round' and as a consequence discovered America. Ptolemy's contribution cannot be understated as many of his calculations have proven to be spectacularly accurate. For example, he calculated the distance of the moon from the earth to be 29.5 times the earth's diameter. The current calculation with all our sophisticated instruments is 30.2! The journey of classical thought continued but Christian intellectualism, obviously influenced by Christ and his teachings, increasingly dominated the evolution of thought within Europe and the European colonies. Then came the invaluable contributions of St Thomas Aquinas. He was the first to integrate Aristotle's classical philosphy with the Christian intellectualism of the time. The name given to his line of reasoning was Thomism, named after him. He realised that there could be a co-existence of physics and metaphysics and for a time his great work the Summa (considered as a literary work only second in importance to the Bible) achieved that union.

Further Revelations

However the steady march of events that, in 1492, led to Columbus testing out Ptolemy's (and others') hypothesis kept the evolution of science looking for its rightful place in the consciousness of man. Columbus' discovery was to eventually threaten the prevailing orthodoxy of the time as Europe was shaken by this undiscovered wilderness. The new continent (America) had to be incorporated into the existing world-view: it created a turbulence such that it begged the question 'if an immense continent could lie beyond our immediate perception and knowledge, what else might be lying undiscovered?' The limits of the known world had now been smashed. The revelation of America introduced the possibility of substantial ignorance into the human mind as it exposed the incompleteness of all previous models of the world. The refined, subtle, wonderfully complex systems of Aristotle, Ptolemy and Aquinas were now found to be incomplete - the revelations that now came with Columbus suggested we might scarcely know anything at all. It is probably at this moment that the systems of antiquity were first wrestled to the ground and that doubt replaced certainty.

Two books published in 1543 were to further call into question all that had gone before. The first was called 'On Fabric of the Human Body' by Andreas Vesalius and studied man as an empirically observed anatomical phenomenon. This was a return to the Greek medical tradition. Its primary significance is that it brought a humane perspective to the 'things' of the world. Up to this point in history things were viewed more as symbolic representations and so there was no real search for a deeper meaning. It is then that the cold, clear-eyed classicalism of the Renaissance era started moving away from the visionary, dreamy, unity of Middle Ages as prescribed by Aquinas. However it was the other book that fundamentally changed the world. It literally shifted the ground underneath the feet of humankind. It was written by Nicholas Copernicus, who was a conservative disciple of Ptolemy as well as an adherent to Aristotelian physics. His book was highly technical and mathematical. Like Ptolemy's, his work could perfectly well be looked at either as a tool or as a literal description. This ambiguity is what was to save Copernicus from the persecution that would be later imposed on his followers. The authorities were free to interpret his book as a simply useful model, one that worked as a predictive and descriptive mechanism but did not claim the status of absolute 'truth'.

The Copernican system replaced geostasis (the notion of a stationary earth) with heliostasis, a stationary sun and geocentrism (a central earth) with heliocentrism (a central sun). The system he thus created had a clarity which surpassed anything that had gone before. Copernicus was able to compute distances and time that had previously seemed far beyond the reach of human knowledge, far beyond even the reach of Ptolemy. For the sake of balance and accuracy it needs be said that Johannes Kepler, a contemporary of Copernicus, eventually got the system devised by Copernicus to work fully. The Copernicus model was about to depose the old Gods of classical romantic thought represented by Aristotle as well as the integrationism of Aquinas. And what was to follow would be taken even further by the genius of Galileo and Isaac Newton.

Even the protestant radicals leading the charge for reformation felt threatened by Copernicus' model and described him as 'an upstart astrologer'. His model turned the whole Christian drama, as previously understood, on its head. Up to this point the Aristotelian thought posited that we (humans) were the purpose, the point of it all, the rational axis on which the whole drama of life spun. Putting the sun at the centre and the earth merely amongst the other planets undermined all previous thought and the many philosophical perspectives that had been built around humankind's 'central significance'. Once this Copernican thread was pulled, Aristotelian/Thomist physics started to unravel. Over the next 100 years this thread was indeed pulled without mercy. A term coined by the mathematician Nicolo Tartaglia in the 16th century –'Scientia Nuova' - was used by the intellectuals of the 17th century and it is what we have now come to call simply 'science'. "Nuova" (new) was the relevant adjective to describe what was happening at that time. It was all blisteringly new and breathtaking!

The Role of Mathematics – Science's New Language

Another key part of this evolution and revolution that deserves recognition, as it was pivotal to events at the time, is the revitalisation of mathematics, science's own language. The introduction of Arabic numerals into Europe upgraded what had gone before. This Arabic system in fact was originally derived from India, and then passed through the Arab world and on into Spain. The irony here is it was the Muslim occupation of southern Spain that led to the introduction of modern numerals into Europe. This included the invaluable innovation of the number zero, yet it was the Spanish monarchs Ferdinand and Isabella of Spain, the patrons of the new world (who had financed Columbus' trip) who actually drove the Arabs out of Spain in 1492. So it was the Arab genius that had devised the primary language of science but the decline of their power and influence left them as second hand beneficiaries of the revolution that they had written the text for! Once numbers had taken on their modern form they became instruments of almost bewildering power. The combination of Scientia Nuova and mathematics as composed by the Arabs offered a magic never before seen.

The New Technologies

As well as maths, science also needed the age's rapidly developing technological skills. There is a slight paradox here as technology is essentially an application of science; therefore one would expect it to come second. However the craftsmen of the Middle Ages and the Renaissance devised technologies that in fact, preceded and inspired the science we embrace today. Technology's contribution began in the fourteenth century when the counterpoise clock was invented in Germany and from there, public timepieces rapidly spread throughout Europe, replacing the old systems of hourglasses and sundials. Subjective time, our own private sense of time, became subordinate to a more precise, objective measure. Our obedience to time was born.

Maps came later, in the sixteenth century. Just as clocks, they changed our perception and experience: maps got us thinking beyond the next hill or body of water. These two technologies like mathematics were to become co-stars in science's ascent. Clocks fixed time and maps contained space and so the human understanding of and relationship with time and space began to change. The full impact of both wasn't truly felt until the 20th century, as the benefits of clocks and maps began as the privilege of a wealthy elite. It wasn't really until the industrial development that these two instruments became the foundation of every life. That foundation was laid in the 17th century and was heavily influenced by Isaac Newton's contribution.

The Genius of Galileo

As astounding and life-changing as these two technologies were, nothing, at that time, matched the telescope's impact on consciousness and society. Some debate surrounds the invention of the telescope as some claim its invention goes back to the middle ages; some say it was invented in Holland, others say Italy. However, although the moment and place of its conception remain unclear, there's no doubt that it had little value until 1609, when it found its way into the hands of the genius of Galileo, the great astronomer and physicist. The reason this moment in time is so crucial and can be argued to be the moment of science's birth, is because it was the point when many 'things' converged. The moment in time when all that had gone before could now be viewed and tested, in a way that had probably never been imagined. Scientia Nuova was now throwing down its first serious challenge to religion and faith which led to cries of blasphemy.

Galileo's impact began before the telescope in 1604 when he proved that a new star had emerged in the heavens. This had previously been thought to be impossible according to the Aristotelian view of the cosmos: his model had described the heavens beyond the moon as superlunary (beyond the moon), perfect, absolute and never changing. Change only happened here and in the space between the earth and the moon (sublunary). This was first challenged in 1572 by Tycho Brahe, a Danish astronomer, who had identified a nova also beyond the moon; Galileo's discovery compounded the flaw in the sublunary and superlunary premise of Aristotle. The telescope sealed Aristotle's fate and indeed ours when Galileo saw the moon. He went on to calculate, with an accuracy endorsed by today's measurements, the heights of the mountains on the moon. He discovered the moons of Jupiter and countless new stars. By observing a secondary illumination on the moon, he worked out the earth shined, like other planets. In fact, Galileo discovered what we now call the universe.

Initially these discoveries were greeted with excitement, as these were the liberal minded years of the late Renaissance and so there was a temporary lull in the defensive furore surrounding the old wisdom. This was demonstrated by Cardinal Maffeo Barberini writing a poem in praise of Galileo, the irony here is that when he became Pope it was he who ordered Galileo's trial by the inquisition on charges of heresy!

It's worth pointing out that the growing power struggle between 'new science' and orthodoxy was further complicated by the new humanism of the Renaissance which was also questioning the value of science. The poet Petrarch

(1304-1374 – often referred to as the Father of Humanism) questioned at the time "even if all this knowledge being unearthed was true what value did it have in creating a happy life?" This question echoes throughout the ages right up to the present time. When Albert Einstein's wife was asked whether she understood the theory of relativity she replied: "Oh no, he has explained it to me many times, but it is not necessary for happiness". Her comments echoed the melancholy of Petrarch. He saw science in its pessimistic and inhumane form and feared the journey it would take us on. Was he right?

But at the time in the liberal climate of Renaissance Catholicism, science was initially tolerated, indulged and at times even admired. The honeymoon did not last long! The Jesuit intellectuals in particular feared the consequences of Galileo's discourses and what was to become his insistence that the sun was indeed "at the centre", as stated by Copernicus. The real problem with Galileo was that he was not merely dabbling in stars and planets; he was also conducting experiments with gravity and kinetics, as well as speculating about the nature of matter. In fact, the first theory of relativity came from him and it was from his physics, rather than his astronomy that the most threatening challenges to authority emerged.

CHAPTER 2:
THE BATTLE FOR THE CROWN

The religious battles were raging in the background between the Jesuits (the fiercest, purest and most zealous defenders of Christian orthodoxy) the Protestants and Catholics. Aquinas' legacy was at the centre of the conflict during the period of the Reformation and Counter-reformation. It was during these disputes in the 16th century that theology, once Queen of the medieval sciences, was to relinquish her crown to physics, the new science. That crown has never been reclaimed.

The Jesuits increasingly felt they had to fight the liberal leanings of Pope Urban. This was the age of the Thirty Years War and protestant Swedish King Gustav Adolphus was rampaging southward through Europe. Pope Urban felt obliged to succumb to the Jesuit plots. Galileo was then put on trial, imprisoned and sentenced.

Four years after Galileo's trial, René Descartes (1596-1650) the great mathematician, philosopher and scientist, published his 'Discours de la Méthode' in which the heliocentric solar system that Galileo spoke of was also supported. Thirty three years later in Cambridge Isaac Newton was grinding his own lenses, in order to better understand light. So religion may have won that battle (in its attempts to silence Galileo) but the war certainly wasn't won.

What have we learnt so far? Firstly that faith, religion and spirituality have not remained static and that throughout history they have had their own tensions. On closer inspection we can also see the role different egos have had on the evolution of all knowledge. It is the ego that probably remains the biggest threat to our awakening. As this synopsis has unfolded it has become clear that the birth of science threatened all that had stood before and so a war not only existed between opposing religious perspectives, but a war began to rage between the great minds of the time and religious orthodoxy. Sadly this lead not only to the dismantling of what needed adapting and changing, but it also lead to an unnecessary overturning of so much of value too! The current duality of our world today bears testimony to that, as I would argue we move ever closer to a 'soul-less' existence. The fear that emerged from the church and state against the likes of Galileo (and there were many others that were imprisoned for their brilliance and beliefs) served to feed the revolution of science rather than halt it and so its march continued...

The Newton Factor

Newton is arguably the greatest of all the scientific figures, for somehow he seemed to see what it all meant (the big picture), as he brought together all that had gone before him.

He extended beyond the reach of the new knowledge into infinity, which brought about the refining of all human knowledge. His greatness arises from the fact that he was never simply a scientist, his mind worked on the borders between all forms of human knowledge such as, magic and science, alchemy and physics, mathematics and God. Our age is diminished by the fact that we chose only one part of Newton's legacy, the part we now call science, but which he called philosophy. Galileo observed, analysed and saw the cultural/religious crisis he had precipitated with amazing clarity. But Newton actually imagined and described such a universal system that even today the accuracy of so much that he conceived is still relevant. Observation and theory had provided the beginning of the 'new order'; Galileo could be described as the match, but Newton was to become the fuel. His work around gravity and the laws of motion, time and space were to completely revolutionize the way we looked at and understood reality. He took the work of Copernicus and Kepler to a whole new level introducing velocity and gravity to the orbits of the planets and therefore redefining our understanding of the universe. His system and the mathematics he invented to describe it, are one of the greatest achievements of human imagination. And even though our current understanding of quantum physics has exposed cracks and imperfections in the Newtonian laws, the fact remains we owe Sir Isaac Newton a great debt.

It is a shame that his metaphysical approach to life has not left its mark in the same way. It is worth noting that Newton did not see science as merely a series of observations. For him, speculation borne of imagination took precedence over experiment and observation. An excellent example of imagination triumphing over experimentation was when Newton was vindicated by Edmund Halley who, in 1758, had used Newtonian mathematics to predict the period of a comet (Halley's Comet), which was seventy five and half years. He was precisely right, and an awe-struck world could see the human mind had encompassed the future by explaining the heavens. Beneath the revolutionary mathematics of both Galileo and Newton lies a beautiful simplicity. They both worked on the underlying premise that nature was efficient, which was also an Aristotelian idea, that nature did nothing in vain, nothing was superfluous. That concept was also understood and further explained by Albert Einstein (1879-1955) two hundred and fifty years later. The idea of a simple universal order with nature (matter) seeming at times chaotic, but having a 'heart beat' of simplicity as the driving force behind all events, is something that builds a bridge between Newton and, in our time, Einstein. Einstein was described in 1999 as "the" person of the 20th century. His contributions are staggering and include photon theory, thermodynamic properties of light, the unified field theory and of course relativity. The wonderful work of Einstein was busy defending the idea of classical physics against what seemed to him to be the new and misguided developments of the 20th century. Newton was doing a similar thing in his own time. He appeared to be contradictory because he spoke about the certainty of a world based on observation and experimentation and yet he embraced the seemingly 'magical' world of alchemy and astrology too. For him there was no contradiction. Like Shakespeare before him he spoke with many voices. He was described by John Maynard Keynes, the British economist, as "the first of the age of reason and the last of the magicians, the last great mind, which looked out on to the visible and intellectual world with the same eyes". Another insight into the man and his importance can be heard in his own words where he illustrates the gap between science (philosophy in his terms) and religion. Newton said: "we are not to introduce divine revelation into philosophy nor philosophical opinions into religion". It is interesting to note here that for him science should not devalue the metaphysical, the realm of the transcendental. Newton saw the two as separate. He believed you could not look at the heavens and find God nor could you apply the laws of motion to the afterlife. So he did not use science to assassinate spirituality and religion, in fact he saw himself as the latest prophet from a long tradition. He was simply the deliverer of God's truth to his generation.

The Choices We Have Made

Isn't it interesting that Newton could almost be held responsible for the divisions that were to emerge in human understanding and yet for him there was no division. We (as human beings) in fact made a choice: we could have pursued the magic of Newton or the science (philosophy) he brought to the world. We chose science, because we could 'see' it worked and therefore thought it was the 'truth'. What must never be forgotten however is that this was a choice, we adopted a particular perspective which to Newton would only have been half the picture, the other half, having been the spirit world of alchemy, sorcery and demons. In making this choice we say something about ourselves in terms of the 'truth' we require of the world. After two and a half centuries of the irresistible progress of the Newtonian model and ideal, the philosopher, Ludwig Wittgenstein (1889-1951) was to point out, that the fact that we can see the world in terms of Newtonian mechanics tells us nothing about the world, that we do see it however, tells us everything. The thrust of his position was that without human imagination we were unable to take these laws and make sense of what was really going on. Sadly we chose the power and the magic of numbers and the 'seeming certainty' of what we could see. The power of imagination and the unseen has not been fully explored. Many figures have been held up as makers of the modern world but only Newton has truly earned the title.

However despite the 'clairvoyance' of Newton and Galileo neither of them truly addressed the most pressing crisis created by their work. This was perhaps because they believed their 'own' modifications of the religious view were adequate, as neither of them were atheists. For Newton, God had merely set the mechanism in motion and so nature and its laws were doing the rest. For Galileo God had simply written two books: one concerning man's salvation and the other concerning nature. It was another seventeenth century man who saw the problem posed by science more clearly than either. This man went on to write many of the rules by which we still choose to live. He saw that the success of science demanded a new investigation into the nature of knowledge, on his travels through northern Europe he saw the Cardinals gather in Rome during the years in which the church was suspiciously and wearily assessing the meaning of the new science. He was at the centre of things during this time and his name was René Descartes. On the back of a number of visions he felt that it was his destiny to unify all scientific knowledge and over the next eighteen years this is what he did.

Philosophy – A Unifying Force?

If Newton's destiny was to be the last of the Old Sorcerers then Descartes was to be the first of the new philosophers. He is routinely called the Father of modern philosophy and this is probably justified for he created the terms for almost all the future philosophical debates that followed. It's probably only in our time that one could argue that his reign has come to an end. He was born in 1596 and died in 1650, so he just about managed to be a contemporary of both Newton and Galileo since Galileo died in 1642, which was the year of Newton's birth, who died in 1727. Descartes wrote the script for science, although he never saw the full flowering of that knowledge. Descartes was an important scientist, mathematician and philosopher and this made him ideal for trying to bring these huge topics together. The project Descartes embarked upon was to define the 'spirit' of the coming age as precisely as Newton's work had defined its 'mechanics', which he did in his famous work Le Discours de la Méthode in 1637 and through a number of essays that followed. To further understand this point in history and therefore the role of Descartes, it is important to understand that the new science was in fact also filling a vacuum that Christian intellectualism was itself creating. A tug of war between Protestants and Catholics was helping to create a spiritual void as the war of words continued to rage. Protestant Europe was more intent on the private salvation of individual souls than on the salvation of the Roman Church. Protestantism was insisting on a return of the primacy of the bible, which was a revolt against the authoritarian Catholicism of the time. Scepticism as an attitude to religious authority was born because it was clear that 'politics' rather than 'truth' was influencing the religious tug of war and so the seeds of doubt were further being scattered. This was the unfortunate contribution of the Reformation and Counter Reformation. So amongst these conflicting voices of religion, Scientia Nuova was revealing a 'truth' all of its own. Descartes saw that the old physics and cosmology were being discredited and science demanded a new basis for knowledge. This new knowledge ironically was essentially metaphysical in nature because even though science was now laying claim to the 'truth', it still asked of those who would worship at its altar to have faith in the subjective certainty of the scientist's objectivity. This became a perennial question and fundamental challenge for Descartes and every other philosopher: how does the perception of the one who's pursuing the truth affect his discovery?

It's important to note that Descartes, like Newton and Galileo, was a believer but he realised that belief alone could not produce the clarity and the lack of ambiguity which he, as a scientist of the new age, required. He had found a basis for certainty within himself but he had to join this to his faith. The only thing outside his mind of which he could be as sure as he was of his own existence was God. So although he was not able to 'prove' God's existence, Descartes' God was the foundation of the delicate structure of the self. God, for him, supported 'the one certainty' of his own thought. This certainty would become for many a criticism and a flaw in Descartes' philosophy, as 'modernity' became increasingly sure of itself, creating a world where there was no need for

God. As modernity got off its knees and began to walk, the question was being asked, if there were such a being, what role could he serve as man's increasing omnipotence was becoming clear?

Descartes' legacy seems similar to Newton's. Just as Newton was a sorcerer as well as a scientist, we chose his science. Descartes was a man of God as well as a philosopher, we chose the philosopher. It seems that sorcery and faith were considered too feeble to co-exist with science. Here again there is an irony as our brief recounting of this strand of history unveils. A man who believed in God, found that his contribution to our scientific understanding has inadvertently also contributed to the diminishing of God's importance in the cosmos. This clearly wasn't his intention but nevertheless it's what has happened. His encouragement of honest scepticism led to the continued erosion of the previously accepted. Descartes had entertained the pious hope that his own doctrines would become part of the orthodoxy of the Catholic Church but after Galileo's trial and incarceration he lived in fear of persecution for what he wrote. What he did was to place epistemology, that is to say, the study of knowledge, at the centre of the philosophical debate and this would reign for the next two centuries. Some would say it still does.

Modernity Finds Its Feet

It could be argued that Galileo, Newton and Descartes had helped to changed men into Gods. However these Gods were not to have a true sense of the moral and spiritual responsibility that went with that power because the primary concern was for knowledge itself. This deity status was also visible in the mid 16th century amongst the great artists of the day: architects, painters and sculptors such as Michelangelo, Leonardo da Vinci and Raphael – these were men who were considered to be of unprecedented greatness. An age of science and individualism continued relentlessly. By 1700 the primary elements of the scientific universe were in place. It had been a hundred and fifty years since Copernicus had dared to displace the earth from its privileged place at the centre of creation and together with that displacement God too was increasingly being displaced from his former position at the centre of the heavens.

Newtonian physics had now relegated the concepts of heaven and hell to the geography of metaphor. No longer did God reside in a heaven 'up there'. And where now was hell located? These theological questions that once had unchallenged answers were demoted to scepticism and speculation. Mathematics had now begun to replace scripture as a way of explaining the world. Mathematics also became an alternative form of classicism to that of Aristotle. It was the new lens used to both perceive and understand our reality – modernity's alternative. The ancient theories of Pythagoras' seemed to further 'prove' the validity of the new language and yet in these early days of new science an undercurrent of contradiction still remained. A number of Plato's (428BC – 348BC) idealistic philosophical principles seemed to be embraced as Aristotle had largely been dethroned at this point. Plato's insistence on the imperfection of the world of our senses had attributed perfection to the sun, so the heliocentrism of Copernicus and Kepler started to elevate Plato above Aristotle in the ever-shifting world-view. Plato's belief in perfection was more comfortable in an infinite universe, which was largely in alignment with Newton's laws. Aristotle denied the notion of an infinite universe in his cosmology, which is another reason why Platonism as the ancient model of wisdom superseded Aristotelianism. Plato's semi resurrection of, and affiliation to, 'early science' is important because it called into question certain preconceptions, namely that science was only about the 'stuff' of common sense. Platonism is essentially mysticism; Aristotelianism is grounded in common sense. Science could be said to be more Platonic in inspiration and yet is more commonly associated in our minds with the idea of common sense – indeed, one of the more celebrated definitions of science is 'organised common sense'..... But does this definition tell the whole story? Is it not the case - like most of life's mysteries - that the answers are found at the point of convergence? Isn't it true that both mysticism and common sense are needed? Science's own birth and evolution would suggest the answer is yes. However, once again we seem to have chosen one side of the equation, that is, common sense over mysticism. I believe these choices tell us more about ourselves than about the 'rightness' of our decisions.

The Divided Self

Descartes, in suggesting an inner self awareness as the basis of all knowledge, helped to set up a dualism that has cast its shadow on the scientific movement ever since. His propositions in effect divided "us" from our bodies, reason from passion, mind from matter. He believed our true identities resided in our minds or souls, the seat of which he concluded was the pineal gland in the brain. He also concluded that the body was an indispensable companion of the soul, part of the world of matter. However, given the Church's crisis of authority and the pace at which events were unfolding, this was not a message the world was ready to embrace. The 'age of reason' and its claim to transcend the deceptive and inadequate 'evidence' of our senses was moving forward relentlessly. And so this philosophical position was being lost in the stampede. It's worth noting that Descartes' brilliant mind dared to put these perspectives on the table at a time of theological turbulence in Europe. This is why he and his contemporaries at times feared for their safety, should they fall prey to the same fate as Galileo. However, the concept of a soul, separate and distinct from the human form, had long been upheld and prized in the east, especially in India. So, what was clearly a challenge for the western mind had long been embraced by the eastern heart. The 18th century saw the (at least partial) triumph of reason. Descartes' fear that knowledge would possibly separate from 'value' had now come to pass. The more that science unearthed the further it seemed to drift from morality and life's greater purpose. It became completely consumed with the next set of revelations, which, it continued to believe, held the key to complete understanding. The paradox of its findings continued. On the one hand these insights into nature seemed to further endorse the existence of a guiding, creative hand….God: the complexity and adaptive quality of nature, ever striving for perfection, seemed to confirm that there must have been some conscious design. On the other hand science's evaluation of things seemed to suggest everything could be explained with no reference to anything divine. This duality still remains.

CHAPTER 3:
THE AGE OF ENLIGHTENMENT?

If Aristotle embodied the wisdom of the ancients and Aquinas the wisdom of the Middle Ages, then Immanuel Kant (1724-1804) embodied the period of scientific enlightenment. In many ways Kant was an heir of Plato, an idealist who considered our understanding of the world as woefully deficient. He developed a new epistemology (study of knowledge) as a response to the crisis of modernity, where 'value' was competing with the force of knowledge. Kant tried to encourage the western mind to look inwards in order that it might contemplate its own moral and metaphysical anatomy. He believed that all we had were our perceptions and these were inadequate in our attempts to know the ultimate truth, not least of all because we are conditioned by various categories of experience, which in turn shape our perceptions. Kant constructed (re-introduced) a morality and conscience into this age of reason and alleged enlightenment. It's worth remembering for the sake of context the tension that existed at this time of scientific enlightenment. Those who led this movement saw science as the weapon that could slay superstition and religion. They believed that scientific 'method' standing on the shoulders of observation was the only way to attain knowledge. Ironically, as stated earlier, this revolution was largely fuelled by Newton's immense contribution to the age of reason and yet Newton had never intended for God and religion to be undermined in the way they undoubtedly were. Before Kant the opposing voice speaking out against the increasing certainty of scientific supremacy was being persistently articulated by John Locke (1632-1704), a close friend of Newton, who built a philosophy largely centred around Newton's science (philosophy). He later was considered, alongside Newton and Francis Bacon (1561-1626), to be part of a unique English trilogy of minds. Bacon was a philosopher, scientist, lawyer and parliamentarian. He was a significant persona in the scientific revolution. The trio's contribution is well documented elsewhere; I am only touching on some part of this here. (For those who want to take a closer look at their overlapping relevance and influence at the time, I would recommend you do so to further understand their contribution). In 1690 John Locke famously wrote an essay entitled 'Concerning Human Understanding' in which he proposed that "experience was the only form of knowledge". He was educated at Oxford and fascinated by science, especially experimentation which he nevertheless saw as a less than perfect path to true knowledge. So he preceded Kant who would follow some 50 years later carrying a similar message. They both laid down a challenge to the ever-increasing momentum of science as it appeared to them to lack soul – a conscience.

Kant's philosophy is a direct reaction to what he perceived to be the cold, inhumane approach of science. He saw the removing of man from the centre of the universe as leaving humankind 'rudderless', without identity and purpose. The lack of direction and doubt that he saw emerging is why he encouraged introspection. It was 'within' not 'outside' that we would find value. This proposition had at its heart Locke's belief that experience was the ultimate knowledge, the ultimate path. Kant's work has been used to explain and justify many strands of philosophy according to which interpretation of history you adhere to. This is undoubtedly in part because he brought a sense of man's value back to the debate at a time when man's relevance was clearly fading. So whether you choose the more 'romantic' interpretations of his work or the 'existential' and analytical facets of his philosophy that remain today, the truth is that he brought the notion of our importance back to the scientific revolution through the resurrection of the irreducibility of man. His metaphysical contribution however would be brushed aside and overrun by the 'practical incarnation of science', better known as modern technology. This began in England in the 18th century with what we have come to know as the industrial revolution.

The Industrial Revolution – The Age of The Machine

The baton had now been passed from Descartes, Galileo and Newton to Richard Trevithick, Josiah Wedgwood and Benjamin Franklin. Scienctia Nuova officially became science and because it worked its authority was questioned less and less. More cities were born out of the increasing industrialisation as peasants abandoned the land to become urban participants in the new dream. Out of this technological revolution emerged factories, steam-engines, cars, clocks and rockets. So man's success was undoubted and the sophistication of what he could do continued to be re-defined. However, the question concerning the great 'Designer' was still being raised but it was increasingly falling on deaf ears. Science's central role was being considered indisputable. There was now a mistrust of philosophers such as Kant and Hume who had dared to question the morality and 'truth' that science was unveiling. Science was now a wilful adolescent, demanding its autonomy.

The idea that the complexity of nature in all its glory was somehow inextricably linked to a great Designer…God was a premise now only really being upheld by religion in all its various forms. By the end of the 19 century this premise lay in tatters and the foundation for our current world view (increasingly sceptical and suspicious) had firmly been established. Hence the large pockets of atheism, probably larger pockets of indifference and the ever- diminishing band of believers who almost habitually apologise for their faith. However, there are those, partly in retaliation to this position, who continue to bully and terrorise those who would oppose the 'certainty' of their religious view.

As events gathered pace and the Industrial Revolution continued its march the same questions were being asked…..Is it a question of observation over theory?….. or of observation over experience?…..Is it the tangible over the intangible?…..Science continues to battle with its own neurosis and I believe was and is asking the wrong questions. My proposition is based on the notion that 'the whole is greater than the sum of its parts' and that synergy is the answer. I believe, supported by my clinical and professional experience, and extensive research in the area of personal development, that 'truth' is to be found at the point of convergence, that is, at the point where these (seeming) opposites meet. I believe in co-operation and collaboration over conflict. Why should we believe that the truth either exists in the tangible or the intangible? Isn't it possible that both offer a different piece of the same jig-saw?...I believe the evidence says 'yes'.

This synopsis would not be complete without mention of both James Hutton and Charles Darwin. James Hutton was born in Edinburgh in 1726. He studied law, medicine and geology (although geology didn't actually exist then). It was through his observations that geology as we know it was born. Geology as a science was created around the central idea of colossal and continual change. In other words, the earth was moving under our feet. And because we couldn't detect that movement it meant that it was very slow. This led science to revise all previous calculations for events on earth. The biblical/scriptural references to time were being forsaken as observation and reason again dominated. The idea of infinite time to accompany infinite space now came together. It should be said that this euro-centric notion of infinite was and remains a centre-piece of eastern thinking, so would not have been considered new in that part of the world. Darwin's contribution (1809-1882) is better known and as a result better celebrated. His theory was that of 'natural selection'. Darwin didn't explain the origins of life but once it was here, he believed the principle of natural selection took over. The essence of his theory was the 'survival of the fittest'. The genes of those species that survived the evolutionary process would be passed on and the new organisms would by virtue of this process be better suited to the environments they occupied. In other words, the 'best' qualities of each species would be passed on to their offspring, creating better adapted and more 'successful' organisms. Within this dynamic there were chance mutations, which offered variation of species. The slow pace of such a theory (as these evolutionary processes needed thousands and even millions of years to take place) was being more easily accepted because of Hutton's earlier geological work. Darwin's theory of evolution was to do more damage to the religious orders than any other theory that had gone before. This was science's most arrogant assault. Almost over night humans had gone from being the children of God to the descendents of apes and before that, algae. Life's (nature's) complexity was now able to be explained within the context of infinite time and had nothing to do with a Divine Designer at all!

For Darwin, this was how it was whether we liked it or not: it was the 'truth', all else was wishful thinking. We were accidental animals conceived out of a self propelling process of natural selection. Is that all we are? Should we be accepting the limitations of this hypothesis? It's worth noting that Darwinism, although presented as the truth, has not been proven. And although it has many persuasive and some irrefutable evidence born of observation and reason is it the whole story?...I don't believe it is. For me Darwinism is incomplete. It is, yet again, merely a 'piece' of the jigsaw puzzle, not the 'whole' puzzle as it would have us believe. One cannot help but feel sorry for Jean-Baptiste-Lamarck (1744-1829). He clearly suggested the concept of evolution 50 years before Darwin! Lamarck gave us the word biology, but unfortunately for him, his version of evolution was dismissed as he got the 'mechanism' wrong. He believed in the 'inheritance of acquired characteristics' i.e. a giraffe's long neck had evolved to that length due to striving to reach the leaves and this 'acquired' characteristic was passed on to the offspring. This was in stark contrast with Darwin's theory who believed that in every generation of giraffes there were those who had longer necks than average because they were genetically favoured; therefore, as they had a better chance to feed, they survived better and passed on their favourable genes to their offspring. The Darwinian story has been well documented and I certainly am not attempting to re-tell it, there is far too much to document here anyway. My reference to it is simply to offer another insight into how the present has been shaped by the past. The Darwinian and the Lamarckian hypotheses (despite the lack of evidence for his interpretation) have both played their part in driving us to probe deeper into the evolution of the species.

The genetic revolution continued and took on an even greater significance when the Anglo-American team of J.D. Watson and F.H.C. Crick (1916-2004) discovered the molecular structure of deoxyribonucleic acid (DNA). DNA is the carrier of the genetic message and some might say it is the absolute essence of who we are: dark, tall, thin, brown hair, fat etc....: all this data and more is said to be encoded in this complex molecule. For a while it seemed that the genetic revolution would complete man's understanding and further underpin science's supremacy. It's worth noting that although Watson and Crick have famously claimed the prize for this discovery, there were other contributors to this achievement i.e. Fred Griffith, Oswald Avery, Rosalind Franklin and Linus Pauling all played a part. The 'gene machine' has been running ever since and continues to occupy our imagination and research. However, even though there are those who continue to tow the party line and would say this is indeed the final frontier, the latest discoveries made in the field of epigenetics (we are more than our genes – see the work of Candace Pert, Bruce Lipton, Dawson Church and others) and neurotheology (where science meets spirituality – a good starting place is The Blissful Brain by Dr. Nataraja) are re-writing our understanding on these discoveries literally as you read this synopsis! The essence of their insights and revelations is that (a) We have to be more than our genes as we only have around 30,000 genes underwriting all human function. Since the human machine is performing billions of activities, how is it possible if we are simply driven by our genes? In addition, the number of genes of human beings (30,000) is about the same as mice! Even rice has more genes than humans!! (b) Currently there is so much that neuro-science is teaching us about ourselves and much of that relates to philosophies and principles we have largely thrown away. Maybe it's time we reviewed the way we are living and what we deem to be sacred? Ask yourself this question: is our current model of the world working? Has science, beyond its obvious splendour and convenience, truly brought us peace and happiness?

The Final Furlong

The Oscar winners in the history of science have almost always been creators of theory: Newton and universal gravity, Darwin and evolution, Maxwell and electromagnetic fields,

Einstein and relativity. Theory explains, theory predicts, theory suggests new directions for thought and experiment. It is because of theory that we've been able to develop engines and planes, synthesize countless pharmaceuticals, unravel and understand the structure and patterns of many diseases. There are some extremely magnificent and wondrous successes that are down to the 'magic' of theory. Yet it is important that we are not deceived as there is an abundantly full graveyard of theories that were considered to be the 'truth' in their time, only later to be discovered to be very flawed or indeed totally false. The earth being flat springs to mind, and that theory reigned supreme until the voyage of Columbus changed our whole perception of the planet. More recently the great Sir Isaac Newton, who was for many a prophet sent by God and arguably the greatest scientist of them all, has also fallen foul of the mistake that theory is indeed fact. For over two centuries his system of mechanics was unchallenged truth. However, during the 20th century it was shown to be lacking and though some of its 'truth' and relevance still remain it has been essentially overturned by Einstein's 1905 theory of relativity and by quantum physics. Scientists rarely claim fallibility but the facts speak for themselves. Theories come and theories go. Some hang around for longer than others, some die shortly after the moment of their birth, some even go on to be proven to be true.

Sir Karl Popper (1902-1995) is a philosopher best known for his work concerning the validity of scientific theory. According to Popper, the nature of all theories is that they can be disproved, they can never be proved. He thought of science as a kind of lie detector! Once again Newton provides us with a wonderful example of this. His mechanics accounted for a myriad of observations on the earth as well as in the heavens. And as science pushed on, every new consistent fact and calculation hammered home the 'absolute correctness' of his theories. These included the motion of the moon, the movement of molecules in gas, the flight of airplanes, even the trajectory of artillery shells. It would have taken a brave man to doubt the theory that never gave a wrong answer! It wasn't until the end of the 19th century that various observations began to undermine the 'certainty' of the Newtonian position. So observation triumphed over theory. Francis Bacon, a member of the great English trilogy I referred to earlier, would have smiled. For he, in stark contrast to Descartes, trusted the senses completely. To him observation was everything, he saw nature as an 'open book' that couldn't be misread by an unprejudiced mind. Bacon, in a different yet equally important way as Descartes, helped to shape the landscape. His contribution however was a relatively lone voice that gathered most of its influence and momentum after he died. Bacon was part of a line of reason going back to the Greeks and Romans that was mistrustful of theory and revelled in the gifts of observation. It's worth pointing out, having been around in the time of Galileo, Bacon was witness to a world denying observation as it continually referred back to Aristotle, Aquinas and the fathers of the Church. Bacon's single-minded insistence was no less a rejection of authority than Descartes', he just saw it differently i.e. he believed what he saw not what he read!

Let us return to Popper. He felt the cracks that started to appear in Newton's theory were proof that the multiplication of positive cases does not increase the probability of a thesis being correct. In other words, although Newton's theories stood for an impressively long time, we should beware of the arrogance of believing any theory is final. It's not really a question of Newton being wrong, it's more accurate to say that the extent to which he was able to validate his theories at that time was limited. Newton himself knew his discoveries were incomplete. However, it was the world that held the view that nearly 'everything' had been discovered and the final frontiers of science had little left to unearth. This proved to be catastrophically wrong with the emergence of a number of key characters. Let us take an interlude at this point to look at their contribution.

The first in our trilogy is Michael Faraday (1791-1867). He was a chemist and physicist who was renowned for his experimental genius. In the early 19th century he became interested in electricity and magnetism and as a result, crucial connections between the two were discovered and the notion of electromagnetic fields was born. In the Newtonian system gravitational or magnetic fields were not considered to have such a physical existence. They were merely a kind of 'equalising' process that balanced out the whole structure. But Faraday, through his experiments, convincingly demonstrated that such fields did exist physically. It was a puzzling revelation that could not be adapted to the Newtonian model because these fields appeared to propagate themselves in empty space! The precise implications of Faraday's findings were realised mathematically by the Scottish physicist and mathematician James Clerk Maxwell (1831-1879). It was he who, with dazzling insight, arrived at the equations that would explain the 'field effects' and demonstrated the behaviour of electromagnetic phenomena. He even calculated the speed of this propagation, which he discovered to be the speed of light. The discovery of the finite velocity of light had been proven by Ole Rømer in 1676 but it was Maxwell who understood its significance and unified it with the electromagnetic spectrum. He recognised that electricity, magnetism and light were all manifestations of the same phenomenon: the electromagnetic field. The fact that light did have such a velocity always and everywhere was to become one of the primary underpinnings of physics in the 20th century. This is why Einstein said in 1930 that "Maxwell was the greatest unifying influence in science since Newton". So the influence of Maxwell and Faraday pointed to a deeper realm and a range of phenomena, which was simply not acknowledged by the Newtonian system. Although it was Einstein who would finally overthrow the Newtonian view of our world, this process had begun long before him. This snapshot would be incomplete without the mention of the Dutch physicist Hendrik Antoon Lorentz (1853-1928). He established equations of motion for charged particles. When combined with Maxwellian equations these provided rules for both particle and field behaviour. More details of an underlying 'order' were being exposed of which we had no previous knowledge. So the sense of certainty that the finishing line of understanding was in view was rapidly having to be reconsidered. The conceptual shock of these events would go on to reverberate for the next hundred years. Some could legitimately argue they are still reverberating now.

This period of history would be incomplete without some reference to Albert Einstein (1879-1955). In 1905 Albert Einstein published four papers. All four were revolutionary but the third –'On the Electrodynamics of Moving Bodies' contained the special theory of relativity. Ten years later Einstein produced his general theory and the scientific landscape was once again transformed beyond measure. Einstein abandoned the Newtonian concepts of absolute time and space as being separate phenomena and unified them. His theory described space and time as different aspects of the same reality, forming a continuum that curved and enveloped itself. Gravity was a distortion of this continuum caused by the presence of mass. It is this marriage of mass and energy with the magical constant of light that produced his formula $E=MC^2$ and would redefine the boundaries of our understanding. Relativity was to change our understanding both of the very small and the very large. These discoveries were again illuminating that science was not the 'road to truth' or the 'panacea for all ills'. Niels Bohr (1885-1962), one of the greatest architects of quantum theory said: "it is wrong to think that the task of physics is to find out how nature is. Physics concerns what we can say about nature". The objective eye could see a humbling of science in the face of these discoveries and yet when we look at the practical applications of science, it is obvious that no such humbling has taken place.

It's interesting to note that, despite the revolution that ensued, Einstein himself was a classicist almost to the point of obsession and so his view was that he had done nothing more than add to the very well laid foundations of science. He had built on Newton's work, not overthrown it. He believed the world behaved according to the classical notions of causality and consistency. Every effect had a cause that could potentially be ascertained and the same physical laws applied throughout the universe. A lot of this was not new i.e.

the belief that the world was accessible to human reason. He did however bring a perspective never seen before and that, combined with his humanistic passion and the strangeness of his insights, led to him being so emblematic: for many, a modern day genius.

The story from here has many more twists and turns but my point I believe has been made...science is not infallible and we must be suspicious of anything that suggests otherwise. Valuable? Useful? Life-changing? Almost certainly yes but it has also mislead us (I am not suggesting intentionally) from the truth about ourselves, as far as we are able to know that. For those who want to take a closer look at Einstein's influence and those who were pivotal at the time, references abound as much has been written. For further exploration, others to consider include: Arthur Eddington, Max Planck, Peter Atkins, Werner Heisenberg, Lewis Fry Richardson, to name a few.

CHAPTER 4: THE BIRTH OF PSYCHOANALYSIS

Although there have been many spectacular failures along the way, science was forgiven most of these because it delivered in so many other ways. By the end of the 19th century (post Darwin) as I've said, there was an arrogance which led to the belief that most of the substantial truths were now known, and that only a refinement of the current revelations was needed. As seemingly all frontiers had been crossed and there was little way to go, attention turned to the mind, the generator of all this reason and discovery.

And so psychoanalysis was born. Its creator Sigmund Freud (1856-1939) saw psychoanalysis as the continuation of scientific endeavour. In fact he would become irate if this discipline was labelled as anything but scientific. When Havelock Ellis described him as an artist and not a scientist, Freud was furious and described this attitude as 'the most refined amiable form of resistance, calling me a great artist in order to injure the validity of our scientific claims'. Freud saw himself quite clearly as the inheritor of the scientific vision and impulse of Newton and Darwin. Freud famously wrote, 'Man's observation of the great astronomical regions not only furnished him with a model for introducing order into his life, but gave him the first point of departure for doing so". He already thought that it was possible to understand the final frontier (the mind) through the lens of what had been unearthed about the physical universe. So he began his scientific search for causality and origins into the drives of the individual. His most recognisable contribution is the elaborate bridge he built between the adult and the 'drama' of childhood. He started by studying pathological conditions and moved on to what he saw as the universal drama of the self as a series of conflicts through which we are obliged to pass to attain any degree of stable maturity. The human self in Freud's hands developed a stratosphere all of its own which he posited was: id, ego and superego. The conscious mind became a very thin layer resting upon the raging storms of the sub-conscious mind, which itself could be accessed through dreams and analysis. The debate around the value of Freud's contribution continues to rage but some of his observations and reasoning have no doubt been useful to our understanding. What is equally true is that he also describes human existence as being a triple misfortune. Just as Darwin's assessment of man's lot was somewhat diminishing of our value, fatalistic Freud saw us not only as feeble in the face of nature's superior power, but our feebleness extended to our own bodies too. In addition, he saw us as living in a state of 'perpetual compromise' as we had to adjust our natural instincts and urges due to the relationships we have within our families, and with the state and society.

The paradox of Freud's contribution is that on the one hand

he claims his philosophy and ideology have a scientific basis and yet the conclusions he draws fall outside the typical boundaries of scientific validation. For example : "Freud's narrative of the self and his methods conclude that if one is to achieve happiness then the route via which it might be achieved is unique for each person. There is no golden rule and so we each have to work out how we can be saved if indeed we can"....Hardly encouraging or hopeful! And if we accept such a hypothesis the question remains: how were such conclusions 'scientifically' arrived at? Yet despite the lack of optimism we can draw from some of Freud's conclusions, psychoanalysis and its various offsprings have unquestionably offered a valuable paradigm for examining the human condition from the inside and not purely from the outside. So while, whether Freud's work truly qualifies as science is debatable, the fact remains he saw his work as the climax of a scientific tradition of sceptical enquiry which had begun 250 years earlier with Descartes. He felt his work went on to confront and explore the true nature of the self and develop further the epistemology of the great sceptic Descartes.

The Finishing Line?

The story I have tried to tell is essentially about the erosion and the demise of the self in the face of science's rise to supremacy. Along the way we've heard voices like Descartes, Kant and Hume fighting for balance as the self comes under repeated assaults by science's growing belief that it is the new bastion of truth. Anything that hasn't been able to stand up to its scrutiny (observation and reason) has been cast aside.

Faith and religion began to show cracks at the point of Galileo's defining contribution, which is why at the time Galileo fell foul of the fear that his discovery would threaten all existing beliefs, which has proven to be the case. In the face of the emerging cracks, faith and religion tried desperately to maintain their dominion. But despite the best efforts of the Church and the fundamentalists, science continued to increase its market share to such an extent that both in the 20th century and now in the 21st century it reigns supreme, dominating our world-view. However, despite science's rise to the pinnacle of human understanding, let's not forget that nearly all of science's theories have had their seeming 'invincibility' exposed as flawed, incomplete or inexact. The mechanical insights of Newtonian physics have cracked and are heavily haemorrhaging under the gaze of quantum physics. Quantum physics has taken us deeper into the realm of the invisible, beyond the atom, and is slowly changing our understanding of the self and our environment. One cannot deny that science's gifts to us are many, however, its threats to our self-preservation are ever-mounting: the atom bomb and the greenhouse effect spring to mind as examples of the destructive expression of science. In our pursuit of understanding and truth, have we gone too far in the wrong direction? Are we now so obsessed with 'knowing', that 'meaning and purpose' have been lost?

A Softer Science?

As the drive of 'hard science' continues, the green shoots of a 'softer science' that is less pessimistic and less certain in its view are definitely emerging. This softer science is building bridges rather than behaving like a thug. It is more inward looking and soul-searching as it recognises science doesn't have a monopoly on the truth any more than the organised and orthodox religions claimed to have had (and mainly still do). They too were valuable and useful instruments of understanding, but in many ways they fell into a similar pit of arrogance and certainty and came to fear the competition of Scientia Nuova. Isn't it a shame that science and religion were unable to form an alliance? I believe this would have created a better outcome for us all because if the best of science and religion could have drunk from the same cup then just maybe the threat of the extinction that hangs over the world right now might not exist. Maybe science and spirituality would have created a world of plenty where hundreds of millions of people wouldn't be starving, especially when there is clearly enough to go around! Maybe if our principles and values were different we'd be making things 'right' here on earth first, rather than spending billions trying to reach new frontiers in space. Isn't there something back to front about pushing our understanding forward whilst dismantling the fabric of our souls? Where's the conscience in a world that steps over suffering, famine and poverty to reach a prize? What is the prize anyway? Haven't we reached the point where we are now simply striving because we can, not because it's right or has purpose?.....I think the evidence of the last 400 years speaks for itself. I hope this document will encourage all who've taken the time to read it to search their hearts, consult their minds and question the way the world is going. And more importantly ask the question, what can you, I, we, do about it? Like Ghandi said: "Be the change you want to see in the world".

Thankfully, as I said, a softer science is emerging. It's operating under new names: neurotheology, epigenetics, psychoneuroimmunology, various forms of mind-body medicine. Some schools of psychotherapy that are also bridging the divide by integrating mind, body, spirit and environment are also emerging. These green shoots of hope are appearing because despite its domination over the last four hundred years, science has proved to be an inadequate instrument in helping us to understand meaning and purpose. It continues to churn out answers to various questions but has brought us no closer to knowing who we are or to understanding the very essence of our existence. Science's obvious effectiveness means the developed world and now even some parts of the less developed world are bowing at its altar. It is for many the God of our time, the new religion. It, like many of the religions that once dominated our world view, has not been interested in co-existence. So how will these green shoots fare in such a hostile climate?.....Time will tell. What is for sure is we need a new way of looking at ourselves and the world.

It would not have been possible to include here all the characters relevant to this aspect of history. I know there have been some important and significant omissions, such as Rousseau, Thomas Hobbes, Tom Paine, Voltaire, James Watt, William Blake, Ernest Rutherford, JJ Thompson, Huygens, Hooke, Hertz, Marconi, Graham Bell, just to name a few. For those who want to research the paper trail more precisely there's plenty of opportunity to do that elsewhere. My primary objective was not to give a history lesson but to highlight some of the ignorance that lies beneath the way we live, and which shapes so many of our decisions and choices.

I also wanted to illuminate what I believe has been the casualty of the ascent of science, namely the spirit. For me it seems that science, having brought us to this point, is now busily engaged in its own salvation. Having taken its knowledge to new and giddy heights, it has on the one hand, created a more advanced world, and yet on the other, made things appear more fragile than ever. We seem to live in a world that's more confident about its own knowledge and wisdom and yet is more ignorant about its essence, its meaning and purpose. Isn't it time we faced this paradox?

With the fall of antiquity and with that the demise of a large chunk of spirituality, science has given rise to another questionable force, which is the power of economics. Throughout history trading in all commodities, sadly even humans, has been a core characteristic of our way of life but the modern world, with even less values and principles at its centre has meant that economics has become a more threatening force. Our diminishing concern for one another has created a more 'me me' culture and that has led to a change in the nature of our trading and the worshipping of another God: economics and material wealth. Now more than ever we seem to have come to define ourselves by what we possess, our acquisitions, and we equally define others in this way too. Have our material ambitions brought us closer to the truth? Have our acquisitions really made us happier and more content? Look around you – the answers are staring us all in the face.

CONCLUSION

The German philosopher Nietzsche said that life can only really be understood looking backwards but it must be lived going forwards! (paraphrased). I hope you will have a better understanding of the present having peered through the porthole of the past. The purpose of this narrative is not to change minds. Its primary purpose is to encourage you to use your own mind.... I'd like to dare to suggest that if you are sitting in the seat of complacency, possibly accepting a reality you have not chosen, then it's worth getting out of that seat and questioning the 'wisdom' of our age. Question your assumptions, perceptions and current understanding. Is what you believe built on a firm foundation, a foundation that you can call your own? My invitation to you is to doubt even what you've read here, if it doesn't sit comfortably with your own experience. The facts woven together in this summary will not meet with everyone's approval and that's perfectly ok. I'm not looking for compliance or seeking a following.

On the contrary I want you to stop simply following, walking in the 'darkness of compliance'. At the very least let this book be a catalyst for you to go and seek, and find, your own answers. My hope is that you will go on your own quest, your own personal enquiry and not stop until you are satisfied with the answers you find. Go and seek your own truth, not one that has simply been served up to you, either by science or religion. I believe that the ancient cultures were right when they said that 'experience is the ultimate arbiter'. Learn to trust your own experience and in time you will taste its sweet fruits: wisdom and peace of mind. It is from this place of peace and wisdom that all other virtues, insights and true powers flow.

This book does not seek to offend or be divisive. It does however invite you to challenge your current world-view in the hope that you will build a bridge across that internal divide. I believe that the future of our species depends on us finding unity within the self and a spirit of co-operation with and love for one another. I hope this summary of the last 400 years will be a useful contribution and inspire you to take a more profound journey towards yourself....

> "The cure of a part should not be attempted without the treatment of a whole. No attempt should aim to cure the body without the soul. If the head and body are to be healed, then you must begin by curing the mind – that is the first thing. Let no one persuade you to cure the head (the body) until they have first given you their soul to be cured, for this is the great error of our day in the treatment of the human body – that the physicians first separate the soul from the body."

Plato (428 BC – 347 BC)

Plato said these words some 400 years before Christ. And yet it is obvious that even today we continue to make the same mistake he's drawing our attention to! Have we, in spite of our advances, really learnt the importance of the 'whole'? .... Or do we continue to pursue the myth that understanding and healing can be achieved only through the 'part'? .... Can we truly understand anything by looking at only part of it? .... In fact, how can we 'fix' something by placing our focus and efforts on any one area? Surely that means we're bound to miss something? My belief is that we are 'missing something' as we continue to overlook the intrinsic value of the self. The countless external journeys that science has taken us on mean that we have lost touch with our inner essence. It's time to tame our egos and reclaim our relationship with the spirit. Science is invaluable, of that there is no doubt, but it is only 'part' of the story so let us not make it our God.... The journey of the spirit is a different journey that science may be able to help us with but it almost certainly will not have all the answers. Therefore I believe we need to open our minds to other avenues of discovery. I'm sure that if you listen to your heart you'll find those paths that are right for you.

The Eastern Story

It's important from the point of balance and perspective to state that the story as far as the Eastern world is concerned is a different one. There has not been the same dethroning of faith in the name of science. There has been and continues to be a far better co-existence. We will look at that story in the next book so that the great commentators and contributors of the East are not lost in the telling of a largely Eurocentric version of history because, albeit in different ways, eastern science and philosophy have played no lesser a part in human evolution. Great minds such as Patanjali, Lao Chi Tzu, Confucius, Buddha just to name a few, are giants on the human stage and what will become clear in the telling of this tale (see Antiquity Comes Full Circle) is that where we stand today is heavily dependent on mathematics: this simply wouldn't have been the case had it not been for the contributions of the ancient Indian and Arab cultures. Modern mathematics as we know it was founded on the system they established and the developed world with its incredible technology is entirely dependent on mathematics. So the modern world (the West) owes the East a great debt.

FURTHER READING

'Science…the New God?' is deliberately written in a non-academic style. It is not a typical piece of research as defined by modern-day parameters. It is an extensive commentary on how I believe science has been escorted by the ego of humankind to a precarious place in history. From my perspective, this is largely the result of looking 'out' into the world for our answers, having neglected to look 'into' ourselves. The imbalances that this has caused have been many and we have been and are still paying the price for that: socially, politically, economically, psychologically and spiritually. The purpose of this document is hopefully to 'awaken' the individual from the slumber of ignorance that the world appears to be caught up in. I believe it goes far enough to illuminate my point. However, there will be those who, understandably, may want to look more closely at this subject and perhaps question/query my hypothesis and so the following material may be helpful to that end.…

Summa Theologica. **Thomas Aquinas**

The Human Condition. **Hannah Arendt**

The World Within the World. **John D Barrow**

Theories of Everything. **John D Barrow**

Causality and Chance in Modern Physics. **David Bohm**

Ecology in the Twentieth Century. **Anna Bramwell**

The Wisdom of Sciencel. **Hanbury Brown**

The Tao of Physics. **Fritjof Capra**

The Birth of a New Physics. I. **Bernard Cohen**

The Origin of Species. **Charles Darwin**

The Blind Watchmaker. **Richard Dawkins**

The Selfish Gene. **Richard Dawkins**

A Brief History of Time. **Stephen W Hawkin**

The Life and Work of Sigmund Freud. **Ernest Jones**

Where is Science Going? **Max Planck**

The Impact of Science on Society. **Bertrand Russell**

Descartes : The Project of Pure Inquiry. **Bernard Williams**

The Quantum Self. **Danah Zohar**

ABOUT THE AUTHOR

Easton Hamilton is the Director of Reach and the founder of The Reach Approach. Reach is a psychotherapy and personal development practice based in the UK. This is an organisation that has been running for over 20 years and specialises in all aspects of mental health, self-improvement and various mind-body programmes. The primary premise of the organisation is that the mind cannot be properly fixed without meeting the needs of the body and the body cannot be properly fixed without meeting the requirements of the mind. Easton has worked in the field of mental health and personal development for over 30 years. After more than a decade of working with very challenging issues such as: domestic violence, drug and alcohol addiction, sexual abuse and self-harm, as well as with client groups including: asylum seekers, those fleeing war and violence and those with severe mental health problems, it became clear to him that so much of the help available only managed the presenting symptoms of the client. In fact, each agency seemed to be more bound up with their specialism or area of expertise and so the client/patient or individual striving to find a solution often was overlooked. This was not a conscious or a deliberate thing; it's much more about the way social/caring organisations are set up. There simply isn't a whole-person approach. In many instances it's too time consuming and perceived to be too costly for organisations to work in this way. It requires much more time and skill and a vision that currently seems to be lacking. This is why he established Reach, an organisation specialising in the whole-person approach, primarily concerned with fixing both mind and body. Out of that desire and ambition a new holistic model has been conceived. This was never the author's plan. It was an organic response to the various needs of those crying out for help. The Reach Approach philosophy can be summarized quite simply with the question – why focus on merely putting out fires.... doesn't it make more sense to catch and persuade the arsonist to give up starting them in the first place?

For those of you interested in finding out more about the work that has grown out of his passion to help the individual find his/her own answers through synergy and integration, please take a closer look at www.thereachapproach.co.uk.

Easton continues to be part of a silent revolution that is concerned with the empowerment of the individual through research, education and personal development practices. Reach was conceived to play its part in that revolution and Easton has always seen that the role and work of Reach is to promote the best ways to achieve self-improvement and personal transformation, which is why he has not made the organisation's work about himself. One of the mantras he conceived out of the mistake that he believes we humans have made throughout history is to 'remember the message, not the messenger' And so he invites everyone who has an interest in these subjects to be persuaded by the message if it makes sense to them but not to get side-tracked by the messenger!

FINAL MESSAGE

We are currently bombarded with messages that tell us that this new concept, idea, product, intervention or treatment is the holy grail and if we only do this 'one thing' our lives will be made so much better. This is a message I invite you to be suspicious of because no one thing is the antidote. Science would have us believe it can take up this mantle and meet all our needs but it too is a false prophet. As wonderful as science is, I hope this brief journey will at least have you questioning the 'certainty' of science. It is time that we understood that science alone cannot offer us that certainty.

In the next book Antiquity Comes Full Circle, I will attempt to show you how we've arrived at a position where we're busy revering the wrong things and in the name of progress have traded away many of our essential values, the very qualities that define our humanity. I will also attempt to show that much of the mess we see across the planet has been propagated by the distortion and dilution of these essential values. If you've come this far, I hope you'll be willing to take this journey too.

The final book in the series, Synergy: The Panacea: The Cure for All Ills will then clearly put together the jigsaw that will increase your self-awareness and help you usher in your own 'age of enlightenment'. If you choose, you could go from this book to that one, because it's not important to honour the chronology: the order of the messages is in fact interchangeable, whichever way you opt to take the journey.

Thank you for your time, interest and attention. I hope you feel this has been a worthwhile excursion.

"A person should only accept a doctrine if his own experience verifies it."

Buddha (563-483 B.C.)

Printed in Great Britain
by Amazon.co.uk, Ltd.,
Marston Gate.